Local Bird

Local Bird

Laurence Musgrove

Copyright © 2015 Laurence Musgrove
All Rights Reserved

ISBN: 978-1-942956-06-8
Library of Congress Control Number: 2015940860

Lamar University Press
Beaumont, Texas

for
Marie-Clare

Books from Lamar University Press

Jean Andrews, *High Tides, Low Tides: the Story of Leroy Colombo*
Charles Behlen, *Failing Heaven*
Alan Berecka, *With Our Baggage*
David Bowles, *Flower, Song, Dance: Aztec and Mayan Poetry*
Jerry Bradley, *Crownfeathers and Effigies*
Kevin K. Casey, *Four-Peace*
Terry Dalrymple, *Love Stories, Sort Of*
Chip Dameron, *Waiting for an Etcher*
Robert Murray Davis, *Levels of Incompetence: An Academic Life*
William Virgil Davis, *The Bones Poems*
Jeffrey Delotto, *Voices Writ in Sand*
Gerald Duff, *Memphis Mojo*
Ted L. Estess, *Fishing Spirit Lake*
Mimi Ferebee, *Wildfires and Atmospheric Memories*
Ken Hada, *Margaritas and Redfish*
Michelle Hartman, *Disenchanted and Disgruntled*
Michelle Hartman, *Irony and Irreverence*
Katherine Hoerth, *Goddess Wears Cowboy Boots*
Lynn Hoggard, *Motherland, Stories and Poems from Louisiana*
Dominique Inge, *A Garden on the Brazos*
Gretchen Johnson, *The Joy of Deception*
Gretchen Johnson, *A Trip Through Downer, Minnesota*
Laozi, *The daodejing*, tr. David Breeden, Steven Schroeder, Wally Swist
Christopher Linforth, *When You Find Us We Will Be Gone*
Tom Mack and Andrew Geyer, editors, *A Shared Voice*
Jim McJunkin, *Deep Sleep*
Dave Oliphant, *The Pilgrimage, Selected Poems: 1962-2012*
Janet McCann, *The Crone at the Casino*
Erin Murphy, *Ancilla*
Kornelijus Platelis, *Solitary Architectures*
Harold Raley, *Louisiana Rogue*
Carol Coffee Reposa, *Underground Musicians*
Jim Sanderson, *Trashy Behavior*
Jim Sanderson, *Sanderson's Fiction Writing Manual*
Jan Seale, *Appearances*
Jan Seale, *The Parkinson Poems*
Carol Smallwood, *Water, Earth, Air, Fire, and Picket Fences*
Glen Sorestad, *Hazards of Eden, Poems from the Southwest*
Melvin Sterne, *The Number You Have Reached*
John Wegner, *Love is Not a Dirty Word and Other Stories*
Robert Wexelblatt, *The Artist Wears Rough Clothing*
Jonas Zdanys, *Pushing the Envelope*

For more information about these and other books, go to
www.LamarUniversityPress.Org

Acknowledgments

Some of the poems in this collection appeared previously in *Southern Indiana Review, Inside Higher Ed, Illinois English Bulletin, New Texas, descant, Journal for the Assembly for Expanded Perspectives on Learning, Sleet Magazine, Elephant Journal,* and *Concho River Review.*

"In the Garden of my Students" and "Old Lonesome's Way of Drinking Needles" were composed while I was living in Evansville, Indiana, and teaching at University of Southern Indiana. "Invention," "Overseeding," "Syllabus," "Deliberation," and "Dear Dad, please stop sending me emails about Islam's anger" were written in Chicago while I was teaching at Saint Xavier University. All other poems were made in Texas.

Section title illustrations by Myra Musgrove.

CONTENTS

Executive Summary

15   Secrets I Won't Be Taking to the Grave After All

Biography

19   For You
20   Swords
21   Do It Yourself
22   Night
23   Dear Neighbor
24   Cupboard
25   Stop
26   Tools
27   Only
28   August
29   Cleaning
30   The Same
31   Dear Dad, please stop sending emails about Islam's anger
32   A Thing or Two
34   November
35   Assisted Living
37   Big Puddle
38   Snowtime
40   Filming Now
41   Carnival
42   Before Bed

Teaching and Learning

45   In the Garden of My Students
46   Exchange
47   Essay
48   Syllabus
49   Overseeding
50   Poetry Workshop
51   Leaning

52	Why I Don't Give Extra Credit
53	Classroom
54	After Class
55	Creativity
56	Cowboy
57	Student
58	I Don't Ask
59	Companions

Reading and Writing

63	Discussion
64	The Call
65	Fable
66	Out There
67	Bad Times
68	To Do
69	In the Comics
70	Reading
71	In a Book
72	Thirst
73	I Have an Idea
74	Revision
75	Writing
76	Invention
77	December

Here and Now

81	Here and Now
82	The Trick
83	Walking
84	The Meanest
85	Nothing
86	Contact Info
87	An Introduction to Breathing
88	Dear Huck
89	Dear Clementine
90	Congratulations, Huck

91	A Difference
92	Autumn Dog
93	Recommendation

Local Bird

97	My Song
98	Write Me a Poem
99	If You Want Me
100	Barbecuing in the Rain
101	Outside
102	Let Me Be Your iPhone Blues
103	Old Lonesome's Way of Drinking Needles
104	Practice Blues

Wanderers

108	Picture Book
110	The Paths
111	Recognition
112	Water
113	Backyard
114	Surprise
115	Scenic Drive
116	Solstice
117	The River
118	Wet
119	Journey
120	A Fish We All Know
121	Wanderers

Amen

125	Drawing
126	It's 10 pm
127	Dear Saturday
128	Deliberation
129	Learning
130	Calendar

131	Definition
132	We Can Do That
133	Time Out
134	What You Want
135	Who
136	Analogous
137	Reaching
138	Over
139	A Folk Tale
140	A Brief History of Standing
141	Like You
142	If There is Sorrow
144	Playground
145	Amen

Executive Summary

Secrets I Won't be Taking to the Grave After All

I once threw a no-hitter in slow pitch.
If I owned a restaurant, I'd play Count Basie all day and serve BBQ for breakfast.
Habits are in the body, not the mind.

I got my middle name, Emerson, from my great-grandfather.
He preferred to be called Edward.
I like writing more than reading, but reading is easier.

In third grade, I had flashcard anxiety attacks almost every day.
Fred Astaire was just about the smoothest cat as there ever was.
It will always be boys against the girls.

I like to wake up in places I recognize.
Cherry pie is my favorite, but I'll take whatever's left.
The Grateful Dead would have been better if one of them could sing.

If you're ever in one of my dreams, I'll be there too and teach you how to fly.
Every book is a bible.
The hardest thing to find is the thing you hide from yourself.

Biography

For You

I want to live simply
With few surprises
Like the weather out here.
But I'd also like to be known
To make some racket
Nobody saw coming.

Would we still be us
If we could read the future?
We'd see lunch on Thursday,
If the flu shot was worth it,
Say what we should've said,
Less confusion in the closet.

It's late Sunday afternoon
And my wife is at the store.
I'm wondering about dinner
And if there'll be wine.
I'm writing this poem for you
Not knowing why or whom.

Swords

Because I don't do anger well with others,
Even then I had to walk outside
When I got mad at my dad for
Making my mother cry.

Summer in Houston smells like
Burger King and diesel exhaust.

I just turned 8 and it was July
And the grass in my yard
Was like walking across knives.
Crawdad towers rose in the ditches
And standing in one place too long
Was an invitation to ants.
Cars splashed by our house
In the wet tar of the melting asphalt.

I walked back into the empty kitchen
And opened the junk drawer:
An old hammer, screwdrivers,
A pair of pliers, rubber bands.
I pulled out the scissors.

Out again through the front door
I let the screen door slam loud
And walked over to the swords of yucca
Standing sharp near the street.
I cut four razor tips from the pointed ends
And kneeling down on the hot concrete
Carefully wedged one behind
Each tire on my dad's car.

I was done with that.

Do It Yourself

The only time
My dad took me
And my big brother
To the barbershop
He decided my mom
Could do it cheaper
And bought her a pair
Of electric clippers
So we took turns
Sitting on a plank
Lying across the arms
Of a folding lawn chair
Wrapped in a sheet
Held tight on the neck
By an old clothespin
And we closed our eyes
Hoping for the best
Hearing Dad in the garage
Firing up the table saw
The plywood screaming
Our hair in a pile
Around my mother's feet.

Night

When I discovered my worst fears
Couldn't possibly open the windows
Or bring the loud knock of bad news
I would sit alone and calm myself
Predicting the death and injury of all
Who loved me so they might live.

Dear Neighbor

And by neighbor
I mean any dad
Who recently
Moved his family
In or out upwind
Because I found
That Ziploc bag
You may want
Blown into my yard
Holding two
Wood screws
And the special
Allen wrench
To tighten the
Corner bolts
On the bunk bed
You assembled
For your sons
Which is really
Like putting
A jungle gym
In their room
Because I see
On the enclosed
Instructions
There's a ladder
And I wonder
How the talk
Went down
When it came
Time to choose
Top over bottom
And who got
In trouble first
And what Mom
Had to say.

Cupboard

In tonight's kitchen
There's one bowl left
Of all the bowls
We used to stack and clean.
Yes, plenty of spoons
In the wide wood drawer
And thick mugs still
Crowd the shelves
But these good bowls
We've worked them
So hard and now
I am kneeling down
Slowly muttering
Another weak regret
Cupping one by one
The sharp remains
Wishing a better bed
Than the trash pail
After all they've held
For me again and again.

Stop

I'd like to stop thinking
About this endlessly if I could
But it just keeps coming
Up the sidewalk to the door
Again and again not caring
If the dog barks at the window
Or even if it's just more junk
Slipped through the slot
One piece after another
Making a pile on the floor
That's no more than garbage
To haul out back in the morning.

Tools

Even words get worn out
Like joy and appreciation
Because they got old
Like my great-grandfather
Who built houses
Where people sleep
Who never knew him
And are irreplaceable
Like joy and appreciation
That I felt the time
My grandmother asked
Me to use his dark hammer.

Only

If I am ever
In one of your dreams
I will wake you up
If you ask me to
No problem
Or I will ride with you
On the back of a giant
Yellow envelope
Arriving late into the city
With its mirrored elevators
And taxis and dumpsters
Green and blue
There with you in the dark
When this gang of homeless
Dogs begins to snarl around
And they want what you didn't
Know you had in your pocket
And it's here that I'll
Remind you about
That waking up thing
I am willing to do for you
If you would only just ask.

August

I worry about things
That don't worry about me.
Like trees making shade
With no struggle at all.
The night road home.
My saggy screen door.
And that grass
On the mountain there
I thought would be green.

Cleaning

If I tell you it's been
Three years since I've
Had my teeth cleaned
Please don't tell anyone
And this morning I filled out
Another new patient form
Where it asks about
Four times today's date
And my birthday and do
I have bleeding gums
And do I enjoy alcohol
Marijuana or cocaine
And the hygienist said my
Blood pressure was good
And my pulse was excellent
Do I exercise each day
And me, no a little each week
And she went at the tartar
And plaque carefully without
Too much heavy machinery
Yes, very skilled scraping with
Little pain except those two
Times up behind the top
Incisors and back there on
The lower right inside
When someone walking
Around in my left hemisphere
Must have stepped on broken glass
And I think she said floss
Twenty times or more
And it won't be so bad
If you come every six months
And of course I promised
And then the x-rays came
And look at those deep roots
She said, the Dr. will be here
Soon to take a look.

The Same

When I was 16
I could listen
To the same album
Over and over.
Here's the paper sleeve
And its cardboard home.
Now most evenings
I grab my ukulele
And send the same
Few songs I know
Out the same window.
And every morning
I eat the same cereal
In the same milk
In the same bowl.
But making numbers
Come out the same
Is like when I was 8
And she raised
Those flash cards
Naming us one by one
To stand and answer
Like when I was 12
Lined up in gym
The clock in its cage
High on the wall
The same every day.

Dear Dad, please stop sending me emails about Islam's anger

Jacob has an FBI internship this summer in DC.
He writes well, sat in the front row, and has a twin brother.
He drives his father's old Cadillac and is always prepared.
He knocked on my office door for a recommendation,
and I was happy to do it. The FBI wanted to interview me, too,
so I shook hands with a field agent in the university library.
Jacob wants go to law school and speak justice in Arabic.

Zeinab flew all the way from her apartment building in Cairo
to teach American college kids about genital mutilation,
women in the Arab world, and her love of pancakes.
Afraid of each other, Irish Catholics, White Sox Blacks,
Pilsen Latinos, and hijab-draped girls leaned on their desks.
She told them stories about her husband, the professor,
who brought his young bride to Ames, Iowa, and Aunt Jemima.

Khaled teaches computer science, and in the stairwell
he tapes up posters about next week's InterFaith Expo.
The Orland Park mosque has completed its first phase,
but he said the parking lot will have to be expanded again.
Every summer, he flies to see his parents in Jordan.
When I see him on campus, I say his name in my throat.
His father is dying in a country that is not Palestine.

Adnan lives on a hill in Beirut with his wife and sons.
Tonight the neighborhood generators have fuel,
and the rains are blowing in from the sea and far away.
In his study and jaw, he grips his favorite briar,
lights the fragrant bowl, and the ashes glow.
Tomorrow he will board a bus to the University,
and the books in his bag will be as light as a pillow.

A Thing or Two

I was driving
Too fast today.
Just through
My neighborhood
Going home
For a quick lunch
And I could see
My time machine
Mind picturing all
I had to do today
Easy as you please
And I heard my body
Say whoa buddy
You'll never be
The muscle
You once were
Or know when
The final stumble
And fall will bench
You for good.
Oh my heart has
Such a job to do
Which is to tell
My mind to show
Some respect for
This skin shack
Which also has
A thing or two
Up its sleeve
Like running out
Of breath or
Turning off
The lights and
Cradling slowly
When it's taken

All it's gonna take
From my mind
Deaf to everything
But its own cry.

November

This weather
Of downy vests
And big jackets
Brings on more
Pockets to slap
In search of keys
And phone and
All of those pens
I'm always hiding
From my old self
So I pat myself down
And I'm in a tuxedo
Standing at the back
Of the orchestra
Tapping the snare
The conga and timpani
Listening for a sound
The ear and hand
Can agree on.

Assisted Living

Each time I visit my dad
I have to tell him
What I do for a living.
As we sat over the eggs
And bacon I brought him
The first thing he asked was
Do you have a contract?
And rather than explain
How tenure works I said
Yes, I have a contract
Because all he really
Wanted to know was that
I had a job and was happy.
And what do you teach?
Writing I said and literature
I'm an English teacher.
Do you teach boys or girls?
Both, I teach at a college.
And he put his right hand around
The joystick of his scooter
Backed away from the table
And slowly so slowly made himself
Another cup of Maxwell House.
After I cleaned up the dishes
He said Do you have time
To play a game with me?
Yes I said of course.
So on the table between us
I opened the Scrabble box
And turned the letters over
As he took two short pieces
Of Scotch tape from the dispenser
And carefully secured both ends
Of the plastic letter tray down
So it wouldn't fall into his lap.
After we played eight words

And he was six points ahead
I turned the game board his way
But his eyes were closed
And his chin was on his chest.
After I cleared my throat
And he opened his eyes
He spelled F-R-E-E
For a triple word score
Pretty as you please
And he winked at me
Like he's been doing
My whole life.

Big Puddle

I'm that
Guy who
Let the tub
Run too long
Fill too high
And when
I get in
The water
Spills over
The sides
A big puddle
On the tile
And I don't
Mind like
I should
I just sink
Down into
The warm
Water and
I shut
My eyes
And feel
My hair
My arms
My legs
My rear
Begin to
Float up
And away
Like I was
Flying
Like I was
Kissing you.

Snowtime
for Bob

We wish against the past
When we think winter
Might give us a pass
But as it turns out
The Old Man will lose
His patience like always
And here comes one more
Blast from out of the blue
And whether it's snow
Or the hard sleet promised
For the New Year's party
We've been planning for weeks
It promises bleak times ahead
Unless it was that holiday
Do you still remember
Way back during that freak
Snowstorm in Houston
After our first semester
Back home from college
When it piled up in yards
And kids were throwing
Snowballs at passing cars
And the four of us tossed
A load of snow into the front
And back floorboards
Of your mom's Maverick
And we toured the subdivision
Waiting for the next assault
And do you still remember
We came upon them again
And we slid to a stop
Flung open the doors
And in a surprise attack
Returned with a barrage
Of our own with all we got

Because we were just boys
With nothing better to do
Than holding on to joy
As long as the snow held out?

Filming Now

You know that movie trailer
Where they pretty much show you
Everything that's going to happen
So there's no risk of wasting
Your precious money and time
On an evening on the town?

I don't want the trailer of my life
Showing me everything start to finish
And keeping me from learning on time
The lines for scenes I'm already in.
I just have to trust myself to be able
To solve myself before the credits roll.

Carnival

The big wheel
Inside my head
Is a Ferris wheel
Not a carousel
With its skewered
Ponies and that
Blaring calliope
No, the wheel
Inside my head
Has bench swings
Rocking slowly
Back and forth
And also climbing
Higher than I
Thought possible
Even though
From a distance
You really can't
Tell whether
Anyone is on
The ride or not.

Before Bed

Some of us *go to sleep*
We set the alarm like clockwork
Maybe there's a book or kiss
And we turn out the light
Settle in for whatever dreams
Come to have their turn.

Others of us *fall asleep*
Unaware of when or where
Maybe there's a table or floor
To catch our rest
In any case, we exit limp
And there can be drool.

Children also have their ways
Some struggle and cry
One more story, one more song
They hate to miss what's next
Or fear dark abandonment.

Then there are those like me
Who just couldn't wait
For his mom to say goodnight
So he could begin his dreaming
Even before his eyes were closed.

Teaching and Learning

In the Garden of My Students

Some are rocks.
They've rolled in
hard and arrogant,
satisfied in the heft
and glare of their silence.
Afraid really,
and sinking,
petrified in the garden.

Some I thought rock
are snail,
hard and wary,
burdened, yet determined,
paths of ache trailing behind.
So glad to have passed
untouched
one more day.

Some have given up slugging away,
and dive down
into the damp dry dirt.
Wrigglers in the dark,
they roam unseen,
happily private,
making the most they can
of themselves themselves.

Some emerge more dexterous,
their hunger pulling them
up this flower,
that weed,
devouring green.
They know change is the self
they live to die to learn.
And one or two will wing.

Exchange

I'm conferencing with students
On their first drafts
And this one has taken the course
Twice before and failed
And he brings me only two pages
Of the six I assigned
And he says he's having trouble
With the summaries
And also should he put the thesis
In the introduction
Or just where do I want it to go
And I say it depends
On if you want to start with a question
And then examine
How others have responded to it
And then your answer
Would be your thesis in your conclusion
But then I realize oops
He's standing before a vending machine
And I won't take his dollar.

Essay

Since the beginning of time
Everyone knows in society today
Student writing hasn't gotten any better
Nor is it really any worse than usual.
The sentences are still afraid of commas
And plurals and possessives share a closet.
I don't expect much improvement
Without better nutrition and stronger threats.
Plus, there are far too many sentences
That begin with This or There followed
By big empty boxes of Is and Are.
(Perhaps this student should take a year off
And read books with real people in them.)
And I'm only talking about sentences
Not the paragraphs that struggle along
Between the left and right margins
But miraculously start and finish
At the top and bottom of each page.
Also, I was really hoping for an original title
And just once my name spelled right.

Syllabus

On the first page just after the required novels
And before the list of learning outcomes
I'd paste a photo of me from '73
Scraggly hair and wire-rimmed glasses
And then torn from my long gone journal
Some half poem or worry on the day
So they might see me and not me
Who could be their dad or worse
With these handouts and so much to read
How jealous I am I am almost crying
How much I love them.

Overseeding

In cold April here,
the college closed
by graffiti,
I drop new seed
over old sod.

Students at home
and classrooms wait
for the all clear
and capture of some
sad scribbler.

I water the lawn.
The forsythia breathes.
We can only be
as honest as
the truths we know.

Poetry Workshop

I'm trying to tell you,
and maybe you weren't listening,
or maybe you weren't hearing me
with what you were too timid to give,
but the writing of your poem
isn't the job your brain bosses around,
much less your hand;
the writing of your poem
is that race toward
getting it down on the page—
that you finish it before the tears
won't let you see the words
and the salt where they go.
That's what I mean.
It's riding the fast bareback
to see who can hold on the longest.
The horse is bigger than you are.
So is the poem.
And that's the life you want.
The waves you feel in your bed
after a day in the water.
The horse under you.
The poem when you wouldn't let go.

Leaning

I know you've been told
To keep your head up
But it's also true
Pain rides the body hard
Whips it like there's
No tomorrow
So I'm saying
I know what it's like
To put your head down
Leaning into it
With all you've got
On that long hot summer
Parking lot after work
Squinting to see your car
Out there near the street
Where they make you park it
And you reach for your keys
Hoping the steering wheel
Won't be on fire
And for enough gas
To go get more.

Why I Don't Give Extra Credit

You want me
To give you
More to do
So that
I can have
More to do
Because
You missed
The to do
You were
Supposed
To do
Before this
New to do
You want
Me to do
For you?

Classroom

Some sit in back
Some up front
Some by the windows
Some by the door
Some like the aisle
Some on the wall
Some with a friend
Some all alone
Some come early
Some come late
Some stay after
And say they relate.

After Class

Outside the Academic Building
Two women just out from English Lit
One white and one black stop
On their way to afternoon shifts
Cars impatient in the parking lot
Make themselves new friends over
What they share nodding yes intently
He was a Marine and flew in to see me
We were together eight months
I had the dress and date picked out
But guess what the asshole was married
Yes the other said I know I know
Happens all the time those bastards.

Creativity

The first idea is usually
The best one you'll have.
Not that it's a great idea
It's just faster than the rest
(Which if they were being honest
Weren't all that ready to be
Ideas in the first place).
And don't fiddle with it too much.
You'll just make a mess of it.
Either way, after you're done
There'll be plenty more
Where that came from
Racing straight for you
Way ahead of the pack.

Cowboy

The wild horse sentences
Of my student papers and
Too bad I'm standing here
With a bridle and gun
The boss man handed me
Before sending me out
Into this dust and sun
Because he wants them
Where he wants them
But all I see is them run
Let me run.

Student

When I was home
At lunch today
I heard a noise
In the living room
And a young male
Mockingbird
Was sitting on
The window ledge
Looking inside.
He hopped up
And tried to fly
Into the room
But of course
The window glass
And he landed
And puffed up
Looking hard
Into the room.
And I could see
He could see
On the wall
Our new painting
With black trees
Blue shade
And orange leaves
Ready to let go.
He jumped over
To the hedge
And pecked
At a leaf
And then
Looked back again
Not quite as hard
As much as
Getting it.

I Don't Ask

I don't ask
for much
(not what
my students
would say)
but really
not much.
But if I did
all I'd want
is that
after hours
jazz club
applause
you hear
following
the bass solo
or upon
recognition
of a familiar
standard,
just a little
smattering
of love,
a quick sip
of cocktail,
and that smile
you give to
anyone who
will take it.

Companions

In the darkest night
When the students
Had reached the door
They said, Master
Please have mercy
Upon us and tell us
Why we are unable
To find the way we seek.
And I said to them,
I am not your Master
And the students
Looked downtrodden
Confused and some
Angry at the distance
And time they wasted
Coming to my door.
And I said to them
Listen very carefully
So that you can know
Tonight what I know.
The way is not long
To travel like stories
Tell us in the heavy
Books we've studied
Or difficult to climb
Like the hard journey
You've taken in coming
To my door in darkness.
I can see your desire
For suffering that will
Be rewarded with truth
But nothing is here
Except what you can
Witness for yourself.
Please do not risk
Your life any longer

Trying to find a path
Through misery
But turn to help your
Companions on the road
And see how short
The way has become.

Reading and Writing

Discussion

Today the books
On your shelves
Were having a talk
About why they were
Still lined up there
Gathering dust
No complaints at all
Just wondering when
You would return
To select one to pull
And slowly slide out
Smooth your palm over
Its shining cover
And release again
The pages pressed
Hard upon one another
Or if you would hand
It over to someone
You thought should
Meet the people
You met and became
After spreading wide
And hearing the binding
Creak a bit with joy
As you reached in
And lifted yourself out.

The Call

When the call goes out
From where I'm not sure
I listen just the same
Because I know it's time
For me to take my turn -
Though there was really
No sound or word at all.

It's just what happens
And just what I do
That helps me know
I'm married to the world.

Fable

The mind
is the hare.

The body
is the
tortoise.

The heart
is the tale.

Out There

It's not unlike
Reaching for
The light switch
In the cold dark
Or buttoning down
The collar and cuff
Or turning the page
With finger and thumb.

Out there at the end
Of all the errands
My body sends me
I reach for my heart
When I reach for my pen.

Bad Times

Every story
About the future
Tells about bad
Times ahead
So we accept
The awful truth
And decide to
Grab as much
As we can grab
Before someone
Else can grab it
Not realizing
The stories
Weren't written
In the future
About itself
But by someone
In the present
Who wants to
Help us hear
The awful lie
We keep telling
Ourselves about
How it's grab
Or be grabbed.

To Do

As I was jotting down
My list this morning
Of all that was waiting
For me at the starting line
I looked at my hand
And it was my mother
Showing me how to hold
The tall yellow pencil
The thin line of my name
Walking out in front of me
But when I lifted the pen
It was a note from my dad
That only he could read.

In the Comics

They call me The Masked Scribbler.
I bring good into the world by revising
The misfortunes I read about in the paper.
I break out my trusty spiral notebook
And rewrite the story to save the day.
The burglar finds the windows locked
The councilman doesn't drive home drunk
The wife leaves before the trouble starts
The tornado bounces over the school
The cancer diagnosis was wrong after all.
But it's not that easy, as you can imagine
Because for starters, I'm a very slow writer
So it's hard for me to stay abreast
Of developing situations as they occur.
Another problem is that the characters
Are often confused about where to stand
What to say and why they were crying.

Reading

Words lie down flat
On the bed of the page.

We wake them and ask
What they can remember.

And though we've never met
They know the story we need.

In a Book

I just read in a book
"The problem is
We think we exist"
And I think I agree
Because I think
We are like books
Readers are reading
As we write them
And they may only
Read the cover
Or the inside flaps
Or a page or two
Or maybe a chapter
But look! They have
Read it all the way
Through to the end
And now they are
Closing the book
Walking to the shelf
And pushing it back
Into the space
Next to the book
You are still writing.

Thirst

Complexity
Starts
With water.

Simplicity
With tea.

Wisdom
The empty cup.

I Have an Idea
for RGM

The line
Between the idea
And putting it
Into action is
Sometimes so thin,
Let's agree there's
No line at all.
Let's just say
It's a green light.
The driver
Grabs the wheel,
Hits the gas,
And before he knows
The ramp is there,
He's already flying
Out over the canyon
Wondering if he
Remembered
The parachute
Or no.

Revision

I forgot what it was like
To write the poem I found
In the folder of poems I wrote
And I thought maybe I would
Split one of the lines into two
And maybe move one line up
And make this stanza four lines
Instead of three like the rest
And then I remembered what
It was like to write the poem
I forgot and I put everything
Back where it belonged.

Writing

Under a shade tree by the side of the road
I sit with my mother and write my long name.
Because I am small and the letters are large
I stop after each to see what I've done.

The lines go down and the curves go around—
The pen from her purse is black like a bird.
I sit on her skirt in her lap by the road
And fall back in her necklace after I'm done.

Invention

> *The essential problem is always the poet's,*
> *not the theory's.*
> —Larry Levis

There is a world of readers,
a library room filled with long flat heavy tables.

There is a world of readers,
lounging on soft couches feet up, the cat curled on a pillow.

There is a world of readers,
shelves laddered up the wall, and pages hinged on cotton bindings.

There is a world of readers,
bookstores of candy, glowing laptops, and the nose full of coffee.

There is a world of readers,
unfolding Sunday morning, and children opening the wings of story-time.

There is a world of readers,
and all I want to do is cry, a cello lost on the path to myself.

December

I am tired
Of reading
In this light
But the pillow
Is comfortable
Against my back
And my feet
Are warm now
And the dogs
Have settled
Into their tight
Curls next to me
So I'd rather
Just sit here
And not read
Than disturb
Those ears
Tonight folded
Down at last
After listening
To me and you
And all the world
Singing into
The soft shells
Of their hearts
And hunger
All day long.

Here and Now

Here and Now

Today, I am walking with Buddha.

He is at the end of a leash I won't let go.

It is tight but does not pull.

I follow the pauses he pauses.

He stops when I stop.

He and I are breathing and walking and stopping.

He doesn't have to look to know I'm there.

When we see our house, we know it is ours.

The Trick

The magician
Before retiring
Told the press
He was ready
At last to reveal
His famous illusion
The trick he said
Was to stand
Before the crowd
And simply ask
For a volunteer
To come on stage
And hand over
Her greatest fear
And then to take
That fear into
His own hands
And toss it up
Into the spotlight
Like so much dust
Watching it sparkle
And suddenly
A dove will appear
Flying and circling
Above the audience
Who feel their fears
Like so much dust
Rising out of them
And they will see
Their own doves
Flying and shining
In the light above them
But wait you didn't
Tell us how it's done.

Walking

When I take the dog out
We take turns getting lost.
There are so many streets
And turns and driveways
And signposts and trees
And those other people
With their dogs too
And the cars and the sky
And the sun is going down
And the last time we were here
A cat was right over there
And wait is that it again
Wait in the driveway wait
Wait wait wait wait.

The Meanest
for Myra and Sonoma

My dog he wants to come inside
The kitties wants to go out
They look at each other through the screen door
Trying to figure it out

I'm so mean to my animals
I'm so mean to my pets
I'm so mean to my animals
I'm the meanest man you ever met

I take my dog for long long walks
I buy my kitties toys
They sleep with me almost every night
I'm a mean and awful boy

My dog gets steak and biscuits
My kitties? Tuna in their dish
I even knit them sweaters
I meet their every wish

I know I have my problems
Don't call the SPCA
I promise to be better
I'm bad and so ashamed

One day I'll go and lift the latch
I'll open up that door
But they'll only look up at me and say
Hey, what are you doing that for?

You're so mean to us animals
You're so mean to us pets
You're so mean to us animals
You're the meanest man we ever met

Nothing

When I get in my good old car
Like an old man on a hot day
I don't turn on the radio at all
But listen to the air conditioner
Roar its hardest as I'm heading out
With my old dog in the front seat
Looking out the side window
Because there's so much out there
He hasn't already wizzed on yet
And we pull up to the drive-thru
And yell at the voice in the box
A medium ice cream cone please
That we share in the parking lot
Before it starts to melt all over
And then we drive home again
Like nothing ever happened.

Contact Info

Tonight I called my dad
While taking the dog
For his evening walk
On this Saturday night
Three days after
My mom's memorial
Who passed away
The week before
While my brothers and
Me and my daughter
Sat in hospice with her
And when my dog
Went behind the bush
To do his job I was
On the phone looking
At my mom's contact
Information and I
Wondered if I should
Delete her number
And instead of coming
Back the way he came
He kept going around
In the same direction
So I followed him
But then he followed
Me too and all I
Could do was let
Go of the leash.

An Introduction to Breathing

I heard some of what the Buddha said

When we expel fear
Through the breath
It falls on the ground
And evaporates naturally
So that it cannot be
Taken in as a breath
Unknowingly by
Another person.

And then

When we invite
Compassion
Through the breath
It falls on our hearts
And multiplies naturally
So that it can be
Given away freely
Without diminishing
To every person.

And I was satisfied.

Dear Huck

Yesterday when you barked
At our house guest the yoga instructor
Who had just arrived from Bangalore
To give a workshop at the health club
I wasn't all that surprised.
And when you went at his ankles
In the living room as he headed
To take a shower after his long flight
I wasn't all that surprised either
Though I was embarrassed
When I had to pick you up
To snap you out of it.
But I was surprised this morning
When you slept in too long
Curled up tight like you do
Between the pillows on our bed
And surprised once more when
You didn't eat your breakfast
Even though I gave you
A little sweet potato to go
With the food on your dish.
And I was surprised again
When we were heading out
For your morning walk
And you suddenly stopped
Right there in the hallway
And vomited up a pool of yellow bile
But not surprised at all
When we finally got outside
And you saw that big white pickup
Hauling lawnmowers and weed eaters
And you lit up like a bottle rocket
Running and lunging and yapping
As it barreled down the street.

Dear Clementine

You are that
pedal-to-the-metal
puppy
at odd hours
every night
a lick on the ear
wanting to play
but it should be
no surprise.
No infant
arrives with
any sense
of what
when means.

Congratulations, Huck

You are hereby
awarded this special
commendation
for your patience
and willingness
to share your life
and pretty much
everything else
with the new puppy
who is not only a girl
but almost twice as tall
though you must admit
with temperatures
dropping now
another body
up against yours
when she's not
snapping at you
to wrestle
may be award
plenty enough.

A Difference

Here on the lazy couch
With Huckleberry
In his comfy blanket
We are watching
Sunday stroll by
Our big picture window.
And every time
A pick-up dares pass
He is up and full-on dog
Giving it bloody hell
Like there's no tomorrow.
Yet when a cardinal
Lands on the hedge
To rinse himself off
In last night's rain
Still cupped in its leaves
He doesn't budge
No matter how long
That redbird hops
And dips and chirps
And shakes himself
All clean again.

Autumn Dog

It's dry and crisp here
And the grass burrs
Cling to your ready fur
After hours in the yard
And when I called you
To come on inside
You looked up at me
From the yellow ground
Grazing on fallen pecans
And you ran straight
Toward the backdoor
But pulled up lame
Lifted your left paw
And grabbed that sticker
With your teeth and spit
It out over your shoulder
And put that foot down
Making sure you got it all
Before bounding in
For a treat you are
Always willing to deserve.

Recommendation

Here's a dream
I'd recommend for you:
You're alone and walking
Down a nice wide path
In a forest shaded and cool
And the light begins to fade
Because night is coming on
And the trail is narrowing
And as the rain starts to fall
It gets a little slippery
And you're getting cold
And also hungry
And nobody likes being
Alone and wet and cold
In a place we don't recognize
And then you are afraid
You don't remember why
You were out walking anyway
Or what time it's getting to be
And just to your right
Under a rock ledge
Sits a small brown dog
And you reach in and lift her
Close to you and she licks
Your face and the rain stops
And the morning is coming on
And the sun is like a spotlight
Blinding you but you are smiling
Because it also warms the heart
You're holding in your arms.

Local Bird

My Song

I'm just a local bird.
I watch the others go south.
This is my yard and this is my tree
And this is the song that comes out of my mouth.

I'm just a local bird.
I watch the evening light the sky.
This is my cat who sits on my wall
And these are my roses saying goodbye.

I'm just a local bird.
I watch the yellow fall into brown.
This is my darkness when stars say hello
And this is my house running out of sound.

I'm just a local bird.
I watch the others go south.
This is my yard and this is my tree
And this is the song that comes out of my mouth.

Write Me a Poem

Write me a poem
Without any words
I'll sing you a song
Without any tune.
Tell me the minute
You run out of time
I'll give you my place
At the end of the line.

The mountain has never
Been a friend to the wind.
If clouds are so empty
How do they fly?
I was about to tell you
A story I knew
But then I remembered
I heard it from you.

Due to the weather
The forecast's postponed.
The color in trees
Is a shade we can't see.
The chainsaws are ready
They circle the block
And wait for the President
To finish his talk.

Write me a poem
Without any words
I'll sing you a song
Without any tune.
Tell me the minute
You run out of time
I'll give you my place
At the end of the line.

If You Want Me

I forgot to look at the sky today
The first time we met is still in my head
When I fly in my dreams it's like swimming on air
If you want me tomorrow I'll get out of bed

I forgot to look at the sky today
I want us to see the people we are
When I was younger I loved only me
If you want me tomorrow I'll put gas in the car

I forgot to look at the sky today
I'm scared when the birds are fighting outside
It's never as easy as everyone says
If you want me tomorrow I can come anytime

I forgot to look at the sky today
I forgot to look at the sky today
I forgot to look at the sky today
If you want me tomorrow I can come anytime

Barbecuing in the Rain

When you told me it was over
I couldn't hear your pain
Now I'm standing all alone
Barbecuing in the rain

I was deaf to what you told me
Though you sang it everyday
I deserve what I had coming
I'm barbecuing in the rain

I know you gave me everything
You got nothing in the trade
I wish I'd known you better
I'm barbecuing in the rain

Here's my grill and lawn chair
The trees are bent down low
The water's coming off the roof
The gutters overflowed

Standing in my backyard
I'm drowning in the pain
What you must have felt like
Barbecuing in the rain

Outside

Here we are. We're always outside.
The sky, the sun, and the clouds are outside.
Inside our houses and cars and our jobs
We're really outside.

Up and down
And left and right
All around
We're really outside.

Once we lived among the trees
In caves and huts and even tepees.
No matter where we hung our hats
We were really outside.

Up and down
And left and right
All around
We're really outside.

We're always really always outside.
Our windows and walls and doors are so thin.
Even the skyscrapers are really quite small
Compared to outside.

Up and down
And left and right
All around
We're really outside.

Let Me Be Your iPhone Blues

Let me be your iPhone, Baby.
Let me hold your tweets.
Slide your finger up my screen.
My pixels can't be beat.

Let me be your favorite download.
You know my games are fun.
Let's Tumblr, blog, and like, my Dear.
You thrill me with your thumbs.

Tap me, pinch me
I'm all charged up.
And, oh, my signal's good.
Please don't neglect me.
I can autocorrect, see?
Let's text, I'm in the mood.

Feel free to search my Google, won't you?
I've sites you've never seen.
Sync me to your laptop, Darlin'.
Your history's safe with me.

Let me be your iPhone, Baby.
Let me touch your tweets.
Slide your finger up my screen.
My pixels are so sweet.

Old Lonesome's Way of Drinking Needles
after Nancy Willard

When the cactus poked out of the sand
and its sprouts turned into leaves
and its leaves turned into hands,
everything else turned into needles
which my mother put in her pocket
which my grandmother soaked in a jar

which I drink whenever I can find it
with my mother plucking the cactus
with my grandmother turning into leaves.

Practice Blues

Just because
I listen to the blues
On my headphones
It doesn't mean
I'll be the bluesman
Like I want to be
And just because
I read this book
Deep into the night
It doesn't mean
I'll be the writer
Like I want to be
It takes practice
Daily practice
It takes practice
Daily practice
Like this practice
Loving you.

It takes practice
Daily practice
Though it doesn't mean
I'll get it right
Each time I practice
It's more practice
Loving you.

Just because
I draw these pictures
Flowing from my pen
It doesn't mean
I'll be an artist
Like I want to be
And just because
I wake every morning
Trying my best

It doesn't mean
I'll be good to you
Like I want to be
It takes practice
Daily practice
It takes practice
Daily practice
Like this practice
Loving you.

Wanderers

Picture Book

Once upon a time,
The Sun lost its way.

No dawn to push along.
Stars turned away.

Gravity vanished.
No hands at noon.

Just a bad dream,
There, there, said the Moon.

The Paths

The paths
We follow are
As narrow as
Our shoulders
Heavy with
The loads
We carry
And we look
Down anxious
So we don't
Fall off
The paths
We follow
But if we look
Side to side
And see the
Other paths
Others follow
And took
A hand
Left and right
How wide
And easy
Our path
Would be
Like the sky
Shining now
On the horizon
All around us.

Recognition

When you enter
For the first time
A new place
A room, a home
A city you see
In the distance
Put your mind
In your pocket
And your heart
In your mouth
And your eyes
Will find those
Who know how
To love you.

Water

We think water
Is home
And ice and steam
Not at home.
And ice is just
A jingle in the glass
And steam
An angry cloud.
But I don't know.
Does water
Know it is home
Or does it pray
It might be
Swimming in scotch
Or flying free?

Backyard

This morning
As the sun
Slowly pushed
The colors
Of morning
Up into the sky
The backyard
Pecan let go
One leaf
After another
Watching them
Spin calmly
Down into the
Arms of frost.

Surprise

After it rains like this
After so long
It's like we won the pennant
And we get in our cars
To watch at low crossings
The blood of that rush
The rolling branch
The plastic bag
The door or mailbox
What it feels like
Being surprised upstream.

Scenic Drive

The next low crossing
will be higher than the last.

The lost maples learned
limestone is easy, too.

The road to Leakey
flies buzzard straight.

The Frio flood gauge
thinks she is tall.

The cedars worked
all winter with no pay.

Solstice

As the sun
In winter
Sets it
Also shines
Its last
Best light
Back across
The land
It lit all day
And before
Going dark
Behind you
It sprays
Like pollen
Golden on
The tall
Dark tree
Branches
That never
Felt the light
Like this
Until leaves
Turned gold
And fell
Saying
We were once
Black roots, too.

The River

There is a river
We have chosen
To make out of
Our busy days
And the sun
Shines no matter
How fast we row
Our hearts along
Or how far
We cast
Our minds out
Ahead of us
In search of
What's below
The surface
And an eddy
Is resting in
The shadows
Cool under
The trees
Reaching out
To say to us
Take this eddy
And rest here
Your heart from
The river you
Are making
And reel back
Your mind
Into yourself
And see what
Is resting in
The shadows.

Wet

The circle
The drop makes
After looking down
And letting go
From the tip
Of the leaf
At the end
Of the branch
That waves goodbye
And then diving
While seeing
Yourself growing
In the mirror
Of the water
Knowing suddenly
Remembering it all
The slap on the back
The ready handshake
The embrace
Of those who
Are happy
To see you.

Journey

Let's talk a moment
About what will surely
Be a time for all of us
When we cannot serve
Ourselves in the ways
We are accustomed
Like the simple act
Of sitting in front of
The friendly bowl
Dipping our spoon
Into the steaming broth
Balancing the liquid
Taking it on the journey
Toward our waiting lips
To cool it with a gentle
Breath before placing it
On our ready tongue
Before it spills on our chin
Our chest or lap again.

A Fish We All Know

In a country unknown
There's a story they told
About a boat we all row
While always below
In the darkness and cold
Hang anchors of stone
Sinking us slow.
But then a fish we all know
With a silvery glow
Saw us skin and all bone
And offered to tow
Our boat to the shore
Where we made a new home
From anchors of stone
And the boat we all rowed
When a fish we all know
With a silvery glow
Saw us skin and all bone.

Wanderers

There they are at it again.
We are standing at the window
Watching them pass by
With all they can't leave behind
Already strangers again
Like the first time we saw them
When we invited them in
And dusted them off
Thinking we were all
They would ever need.

Amen

Drawing

Here's a yellow crayon
If you peel
Off the paper
That's the sun today
And the black one
That's the shadow
On the asphalt
Bleeding tar
The green one
Is the grass
Under that tree
Where you should
Take the red one
And draw my heart
Around you
Then I'll draw
With this blue
A deep pool
For you to swim
That's it.

It's 10 pm

It's 10 pm and time
To put the day away
You can roll it up
Like a yoga mat
Or crush it round
For the garbage can
Or like a t-shirt
Grab it by the shoulders
Give it a good shake
And fold it the way you do
There's a place
In the dresser drawer
Just on top
Of all the other days
You may never wear again.

Dear Saturday

Sorry, Saturday, to have put
So much pressure on you
To make every second count.

All week long and especially
Let's say Wednesday on
We plan for what you owe us.

Then we sleep late but pile on shopping
Yard work, laundry, the college game
Dinner out, the Cineplex, and maybe sex.

But do we give the other days their due?
Really listen to what Tuesday has to say?
Ever held Thursday in our arms?

Even when a three-day comes along
Monday is still sad and blue
Because we change its name to another day.

Next to you, Saturday,
Friday never has our attention
And Sunday is a lazy boy.

Deliberation
for Jean and Steve

Climbing up the wooden stairs
from the damp and low hung
basement into the curious eyes

of the worried couple, she reported
that she had indeed spoken
with the crowd assembled below,

presented the choices as instructed,
that is, leave or the exterminator
would be called straight away

(not the choice the wife preferred,
she who had searched online for
child-proof options to traps and poison)

better they should choose another home
or the nearby farm of easy corn.
So when huddled for her report,

the husband doubtful of silent talk,
the animal communicator smiled
and nodded, an ear even then to

the high debate pressing on below,
confident a resolution still possible
even though the rats remained divided.

Learning

Here, I say, like this, I say,
Curl the hose around.
And always raise the hammer high
Before you bring it down.
Like this, I say, watch and learn.
We'll do it more again.

Iron the collar flat, you say,
See how smooth it feels
And always push the drawer back in.
Look how straight and clean.
Like this, you say, watch and learn.
We'll do it more again.

Here's my lips
And here's my kiss.
Feel the way I do.
There's your lips
And there's your kiss.
I feel the way you do.
Just like this, we touch and learn.
We'll do it more again.

Calendar

Yesterday left
Without saying
Goodbye.

Today completely
Forgot to call
His mother.

Tomorrow is
Outside
Waiting in the car.

Definition

What is the name
For the thing
That happens
When the thing
That needs fixing
For which
You've made
An appointment
Is a thing
At the time
Of the appointment
That no longer
Needs fixing
With you standing
There looking
At the guy
Who's looking
Back and forth
Between you
And the thing
Wondering
What needs fixing?

We Can Do That

The official form
Has been posted
For your convenience
Online for download.

Because it is new
And no one has
Actually used it as
An official form

There may be those
Who do not know
How to fill it out
According to what

We decided we
Wanted to know
From you. But that's
OK. When we get it

We'll just ask you
To redo it because
We made the form
And we can do that.

Time Out

There's no time left.
It was all used up
Before we got here
So now we borrow
What time we need
To pay off the time
We received earlier
To give us the time
To figure out how
To borrow the time
Needed to postpone
The overdue time
We will be charged
For being late with
The time credited
To the little time
Remaining to us.

What You Want

Is not going to make you
As happy as you thought
It would make you

Because what you want
Is not what you will want
When you get it.

What will make you
As happy as you want
It to make you

Is what you once had
But didn't know to want
When you had it

Because you thought
It was already wanting
When you had it.

Who

I am filled
With questions.
They pile high
On my desk
And on the floor
Around my bed.
Boxes in the garage.
We easily forget
What's inside
Why we held on
How it happened
Where we were going
When all we want
Someone to say
Is yes.

Analogous

The head is
A smarty-pants
While the body
Rarely gets coin
For all it knows.
The brain may be
Like a computer
And the body
An old jalopy
But when I say
I like poems
I don't mean
This one.
I like poems
Because they
Are always
About me and
Always about you
Which I'm all
About, too
Me being you.

Reaching

I'll tell you what I'm most interested in.
Not me of course I know me too much
But you who I don't know and likely may never.

No telling what you're interested in most.
Not me much who you don't know at all
Still I'm the you you don't know and won't ever.

Tell me what most of us are interested in.
It's you and me who'll never amount to much
Because we're the us we'll never get to know.

Let me tell you what should interest us most.
Though we aren't likely to know much at all
If I reached for you would you too or ever know?

Over

I trust you
To trust
My pen
Over my mouth,
Like I do.

I trust north
Over south,
Even though
The sky here.

I trust moon
Over sun.
Go over come.

All you hear
About me
Fills up
My shoes.

Walk over run.

A Folk Tale

Once upon a time
A man and a woman
Sat in a doctor's office
Waiting for the sure news
They had failed again
With the biochemistry
Necessary for parenthood
While the doctor despairing
Of delivering the verdict
Walked out the back door
Into the parking garage
Climbed into his truck
Drove to a Starbucks
And picked up a coffee.
Then waiting at the stoplight
He saw on the esplanade
A woman sunburned and cold
Holding a cardboard sign
Just left abuser husband
To save my kids and I.
He lowered his window
Handed her his coffee
And reached for his wallet.
Back at the medical center
Reviewing the woman's file
The nurse noticed her error
And prepared her apology
To the doctor and the man
And the woman with child.

A Brief History of Standing

The Qigong master unfolds
A brief history of standing,
And in the mirror I see
My feet drink the floor.

The brief history of standing
Unfolds a vertical man,
And my feet drink the floor,
Rooting into stone.

The unfolded man asks
"Am I worthy today?"
Questions like stones
Root in my heart.

Am I worthy today
To follow the master?
I see in the mirror
My long history of stones.

Like You

I have a friend
I've never met
Who doesn't know
We haven't met
And when we do
We'll probably think
Who would have
Ever known that
Such a friend
Was out there
Waiting but not
Waiting because
We never knew
A friend like you
And such as me
Was ever out there
For a friend like you
And such as me.

If There is Sorrow

If there is sorrow
We know it too
Because always
This long street
Is our street
And the bus
We are waiting for
In the evening cold
After another day
Beaten down hard
Or lifted up high
By the ones we want
So bad to love us
Is just there coming
Around the corner
And stops heavy
And tired before us
And we are now
Standing aside to let
The young mother
And her sleeping child
And all of her bags
Step off carefully
And we watch her
Put him in the stroller
And disappear into
A white mist rising
In the big old middle
Of the slippery street
While we think about
Dinner and home
And the warm bed
We made together
In the morning dark
Before we sat
Face to face

Over coffee trying
To shake off the day
Coming straight at us
Before it even happens.

Playground

I'm not afraid
To say I don't
Remember if
We've talked
About this before
Though I expect
We have but
I'm standing here
Behind the swing
Wondering if
You need another
Push or not
Or maybe you're
Doing just fine
Pulling back on
Those long chains
Legs out front
Toes to the best blue
We've seen in days
It's not always
Easy back here
Knowing just what
You need or how
You're feeling
Flying there
Away from me
But I'm here
When you want
Another touch
Or ready to
Take turns.

Amen

Time is not
A rubber band
To stretch forever
And ever amen.
Or a balloon
To keep blowing
Ourselves into
Without end amen.
No matter how
Much we take on
Or decide amen to
Stay and work late
Just one more night
Or to give amen
Another weekend
To the boss again,
There's no kindness
Time will give us
Until we say amen
To the time we gave
And sing the song
That comes after
We say amen.

www.ingramcontent.com/pod-product-compliance
Lightning Source LLC
Chambersburg PA
CBHW031136090426
42738CB00008B/1108